SandCastle™

First Rhymes

Billy Goat Can Float

Kelly Doudna

Consulting Editor, Diane Craig, M.A./Reading Specialist

ABDO
Publishing Company

Published by ABDO Publishing Company, 4940 Viking Drive, Edina, Minnesota 55435.

Printed in the United States.

Credits
Edited by: Pam Price
Curriculum Coordinator: Nancy Tuminelly
Cover and Interior Design and Production: Mighty Media
Photo Credits: AbleStock, Photodisc

Library of Congress Cataloging-in-Publication Data

Doudna, Kelly, 1963-
    Billy goat can float / Kelly Doudna.
       p. cm. -- (First rhymes)
    ISBN 1-59679-453-4 (hardcover)   4051 3615   6/09
    ISBN 1-59679-454-2 (paperback)
       1. English language--Rhyme--Juvenile literature. I. Title. II. Series.
PE1517.D62 2003
808.1--dc22
                                                                    2005048046

SandCastle™ books are created by a professional team of educators, reading specialists, and content developers around five essential components that include phonemic awareness, phonics, vocabulary, text comprehension, and fluency. All books are written, reviewed, and leveled for guided reading and early intervention reading, and designed for use in shared, guided, and independent reading and writing activities to support a balanced approach to literacy instruction.

Let Us Know

After reading the book, SandCastle would like you to tell us your stories about reading. What is your favorite page? Was there something hard that you needed help with? Share the ups and downs of learning to read. We want to hear from you! To get posted on the ABDO Publishing Company Web site, send us e-mail at:

sandcastle@abdopub.com

SandCastle Level: Beginning

-oat

boat

coat

goat

moat

throat

This is a .

Look at the  .

Here is a  .

This is a  .

Look at his  .

The boat is in water.

The coat is warm.

The goat is cute.

The moat goes around the castle.

This is my throat.

Billy Goat Can Float

Billy Goat has a boat.

Billy Goat has a boat
that he wants to float.

Billy Goat has a boat that he wants to float around the moat.

Billy Goat
puts on his coat
and gets into the boat
that he wants to float
around the moat.

After Billy Goat
puts on his coat
and gets into his boat,
he clears his throat.

Now he's ready to float
around the moat!

About SandCastle™

A professional team of educators, reading specialists, and content developers created the SandCastle™ series to support young readers as they develop reading skills and strategies and increase their general knowledge. The SandCastle™ series has four levels that correspond to early literacy development in young children. The levels are provided to help teachers and parents select the appropriate books for young readers.

Emerging Readers
(no flags)

Beginning Readers
(1 flag)

Transitional Readers
(2 flags)

Fluent Readers
(3 flags)

These levels are meant only as a guide. All levels are subject to change.

To see a complete list of SandCastle™ books and other nonfiction titles from ABDO Publishing Company, visit www.abdopub.com or contact us at:
4940 Viking Drive, Edina, Minnesota 55435 • 1-800-800-1312 • fax: 1-952-831-1632